the times I knew I was gay

by

Eleanor Crewes

SCRIBNER

NEW YORK   LONDON   TORONTO   SYDNEY   NEW DELHI

Scribner

An Imprint of Simon & Schuster, Inc.

1230 Avenue of the Americas

New York, NY 10020

First Scribner hardcover edition October 2020

For information about special discounts for bulk purchases, please contact
Simon & Schuster Special Sales at
1-866-506-1949 or business@simonandschuster.com.

The Simon & Schuster Speakers Bureau can bring authors to your live event.
For more information or to book an event, contact the Simon & Schuster
Speakers Bureau at
1-866-248-3049 or visit our website at
www.simonspeakers.com.

Manufactured in the United States of America

1   3   5   7   9   10   8   6   4   2

Library of Congress Cataloging-in-Publication Data is available.

ISBN 978-1-9821-4710-5
ISBN 978-1-9821-4712-9 (ebook)

Lyrics on page 309 from "Weird Cool" by Lazy Day, written by
Tilly Scantlebury, reprinted by kind permission of the artist.

We form ourselves within the vocabularies that we did not choose, and sometimes we have to reject those vocabularies, or actively develop new ones.
— Judith Butler, *2015*

"People," the doctor said sadly, "*are always so anxious to get things out in the open where they can put a name to them.*"
— Shirley Jackson, *The Haunting of Hill House*

She scissored the curls away, and ... it was not like she was cutting hair, it was as if I had a pair of wings beneath my shoulder-blades, that the flesh had all grown over, and she was slicing free ...
— Sarah Waters, *Tipping the Velvet*

FOREWORD

THE TIMES I KNEW I WAS GAY WAS AN IDEA
THAT SPRANG INTO MY HEAD JUST AFTER
I CAME OUT. WHAT STARTED AS A SECRET
PROJECT TURNED INTO A TEN-PAGE ZINE.
LIKE MY OWN PERSONAL COURIER, I BIKED
ACROSS LONDON TO DELIVER MY ZINES TO
COMIC SHOPS, AND POSTED THEM AS CLOSE
AS BRIGHTON AND AS FAR AS GLASGOW.
ALTHOUGH THE SCALE OF THE OPERATION
WAS MODEST, IT QUITE QUICKLY TURNED
INTO A TALE THAT I KNEW WAS MUCH BIGGER
THAN SOMETHING I COULD FIT INTO THOSE
HAND-STITCHED COMICS.

THIS IS NOT A HANDBOOK FOR COMING OUT,
OR FOR BEING GAY. BUT I LIKE TO THINK THAT
IF I HAD FOUND THIS BOOK AS A CHILD, OR A
TEENAGER, OR A YOUNG ADULT, I MIGHT HAVE
KNOWN A LITTLE MORE ABOUT MYSELF A
LITTLE SOONER.

PROLOGUE

Growing up, I felt like I had a secret deep inside me.
It was as though someone had handed me a letter
that I had to keep very safe, but wasn't allowed to
open until the time was right.

I carried it around for years,
waiting for a sign that would tell me:
"It's now, you're ready."

Until that moment, I needed to be
the best version of myself at all times.
I needed to deserve my letter because, in my mind,
it held the secret to happiness.

ONE

GROWING UP,
I LOVED BEING DIFFERENT.

UNLIKE MOST OF THE GIRLS IN MY CLASS,
I LIKED GOTHS, ROCK MUSIC, AND ANYTHING SPOOKY.

BUT I ALWAYS HAD MY BEST FRIENDS,
CAT, DAN, AND CECILIA, TO UNDERSTAND ME.

I WAS HOOKED.

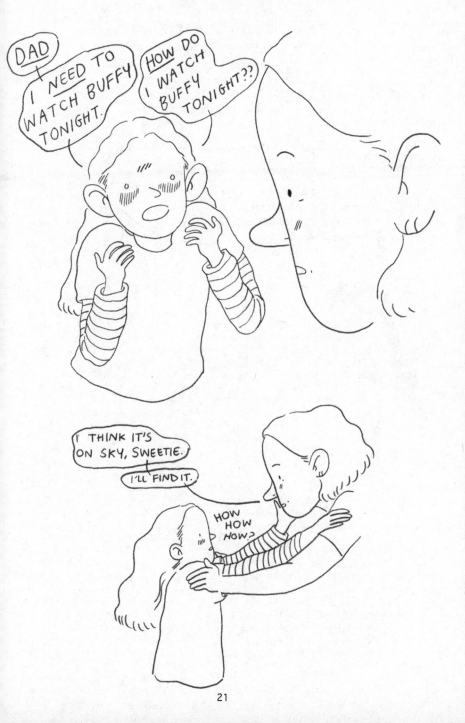

ANY MOMENT I COULD SNATCH
TO CHAT TO CECILIA ABOUT IT,
I WOULD.

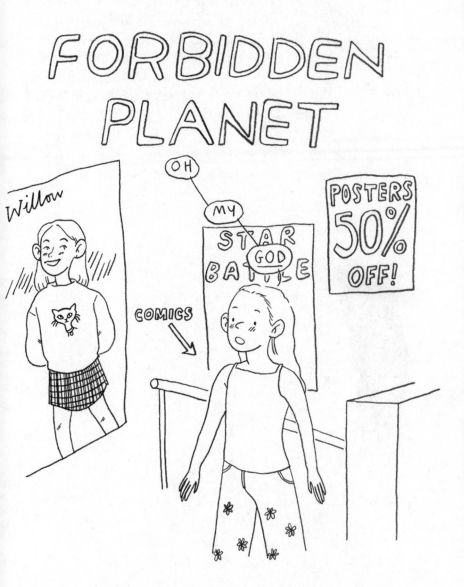

I QUICKLY BECAME OBSESSED WITH THE
SPELL-CASTING, RED-HAIRED WILLOW ROSENBERG.

WILLOW BEGAN TO PLAY A ROLE IN MOST PARTS OF MY LIFE. PLAYING MAKE-BELIEVE AT SCHOOL, I WOULD ALWAYS CHOOSE TO BE CALLED "WILLOW" AND I HAD MY LONG RED HAIR CHOPPED TO MY SHOULDERS EXACTLY LIKE HERS (THINK SEASON THREE, EPISODE SIXTEEN, "DOPPELGANGLAND").

SHE'S NOT ACTUALLY A VAMPIRE, BUT THIS IS A DOUBLE FROM ANOTHER DIMENSION.

IN SEASON FOUR, WILLOW CAME OUT AND BEGAN A RELATIONSHIP WITH TARA. WHEN I WATCHED THIS WITH MY FAMILY, WE DIDN'T TOTALLY ACKNOWLEDGE THEIR RELATIONSHIP BEYOND THE CONFINES OF MY TELEVISION.

ALTHOUGH I DID SIT IN MY ROOM AND
DRAW A LOT OF COMICS ABOUT THEM...

TWO

WHEN I WAS ELEVEN, I MOVED FROM MY SMALL, ROSY-CHEEKED, CATHOLIC PRIMARY SCHOOL TO A VERY LARGE, VERY NOISY SECONDARY SCHOOL.

I WAS CATAPULTED FROM BEING IN THE OLDEST
CLASS TO BEING IN THE YOUNGEST,
AND I FELT VERY YOUNG.

AT MY OLD SCHOOL I HAD THOUGHT I WAS COOL, SO IN CHARGE. BUT SUDDENLY ALL THE THINGS I LIKED, OTHER PEOPLE MADE FUN OF.

35

BUT THAT TOUGH PERSONA BROKE DOWN WHEN I WAS TEASED. LIKE WHEN I WORE THE TRAINING BRA I'D BEEN SO PROUD OF.

I HAD FELT REALLY COOL WHEN MY OLD FRIENDS HAD SEEN IT.

SUDDENLY MY BRA SEEMED SO CHILDISH,
SO SMALL AND SILLY.

I CLEARLY WASN'T VERY GOOD AT BEING GROWN UP!

I WAS PRETTY SCARED OF BEING REJECTED, SO I TOOK MY FEARS OUT ON MY FRIENDS.

IT MADE ME FEEL TERRIBLE.

SCHOOL HAD BECOME SUCH A CONFUSING
PLACE THAT, COME SUMMER, I COULDN'T WAIT
TO HEAD OFF TO MY FAMILY IN ITALY
AND FORGET ABOUT IT ALL FOR A FEW MONTHS.

IN ITALY I COULD TOTALLY RELAX INTO MYSELF.
THERE WERE NO FRIENDS OR PEERS
OBSERVING ME, ONLY MY FAMILY.

AWAY FROM TEENAGE COMPETITIVENESS,
ITALY WAS A PLACE WHERE MY BROTHER AND I
COULD JUST BE KIDS.

BACK IN LONDON, SCHOOL STILL HUNG OVER
ME LIKE A HEAVY CLOUD, TO THE POINT WHERE I
STARTED BEGGING NOT TO HAVE TO GO BACK.

I FELT AS THOUGH I HAD TWO SELVES:
ONE WAS THE PERSON I NEEDED TO BE
WITH MY NEW FRIENDS,
AND THE OTHER WAS WHO I HAD ALWAYS BEEN
WITH MY OLD FRIENDS AND MY FAMILY.

I WAS TERRIFIED OF BULLIES,
THE WAY THEY SEEMED TO READ YOUR MIND,
OR SEE YOU MORE CLEARLY THAN YOU
SAW YOURSELF.

AND THAT WAS REALLY SCARY.

AT MY SCHOOL THERE WAS ONE BOY IN PARTICULAR,
WHO WAS ALWAYS PICKED ON FOR BEING GAY.

IT QUICKLY TURNED FROM A RUMOR INTO A FACT, AND THIS TERRIFIED ME THE MOST.

EVERYONE SEEMED SO HUNGRY TO KNOW
EVERYTHING ABOUT YOU.

BUT I DIDN'T EVEN SEEM TO KNOW MYSELF ANYMORE.

WHATEVER ANYONE FOUND OUT ABOUT ME,
AT LEAST I HAD MY FRIENDS TO TALK TO.

THREE

AS CAT, AISLING, AND I GOT OLDER, IT SUDDENLY SEEMED LIKE EVERYONE HAD BOYFRIENDS.

FROM THE AGE OF FOUR UNTIL I WAS TEN, I HAD LOVED THE SAME BOY. BUT I HADN'T REALLY FANCIED ANYONE. A WHOLE NEW WORLD WAS OPENING UP BEFORE ME AND I DIDN'T KNOW WHETHER TO DIVE IN OR RUN FOR THE HILLS.

THE FLIRTING TECHNIQUES OF A

(UNBEKNOWNST TO HER)

CLOSETED LESBIAN.

STEP ONE:

BECOME THE BOY — MAKE A NOTE OF HIS HAIRCUT, SNEAKERS, RUCKSACK, HOW MANY WRISTBANDS HE WEARS / WHAT COLOR THEY ARE. DOES HE HAVE A NECKLACE? IS IT ONE OF THOSE WOODEN BEADED ONES FROM TOPMAN? YES? GOOD — THEY'RE CHEAP AND EASILY ATTAINABLE.

STEP TWO:

WHAT TV SHOWS DOES HE WATCH? ARE THEY AT
BLOCKBUSTER? CAN I WATCH AN ENTIRE SERIES IN
ONE WEEKEND AND THEREFORE BE ABLE TO MAKE
CONVERSATION ON MONDAY IN HISTORY?

AM I VERGING ON BECOMING A STALKER? NO!
I'M FLIRTING, SOWING THE SEED, GETTING A FEEL FOR
THE LAY OF THE LAND.

STEP THREE:

AS SOON AS I KNOW THAT THEY FANCY
ME BACK, DECIDE THAT IT'S TOO
STRESSFUL AND WHAT YOU'VE NOW
BUILT AS FRIENDSHIP IS TOO
VALUABLE TO LOSE.

THE FIRST BOY I SAID I FANCIED* WAS IN YEAR 8,
WHEN I WAS TWELVE. WE BOTH LIKED READING
MANGA AND WATCHING ANIME AND
WOULD TALK OBSESSIVELY
ABOUT OUR FAVORITE
STORY LINES.

*WHEN I SAY "FANCY,"
IT MEANT MORE
BECAUSE THEY LIKED
THE SAME THINGS AS ME.
I THOUGHT THAT THE
PHYSICAL ATTRACTION
WOULD COME LATER ON.

HE TOOK ME ON MY FIRST EVER DATE TO WATCH
STARDUST AT THE ODEON CINEMA.
WE DIDN'T SPEAK THE WHOLE TIME BUT THAT
DIDN'T STOP ME FROM ASKING HIM TO BE
MY BOYFRIEND VIA MSN INSTANT MESSENGER.

WE DIDN'T SPEAK AFTER THAT, EITHER.
AFTER TWO WEEKS OF BEING A "COUPLE,"
CAT AND AISLING BROKE UP WITH HIM FOR ME.

THE SECOND BOY I REALLY FANCIED WENT TO A
DIFFERENT SCHOOL.

HE WAS SMART — COOL!
HE WAS JEWISH — COOL!
AND HE FANCIED ME BACK — MEGA COOL!

I HAD MY FIRST KISS WITH HIM WHEN I WAS FOURTEEN AT THE CINEMA (THE SAME ONE I'D WATCHED *STARDUST* AT TWO YEARS EARLIER). I WAS SO AWARE OF HIM FROM THE MOMENT WE SAT DOWN IN FRONT OF THE SCREEN.

AS THE FILM PLAYED WE MOVED CLOSER AND CLOSER TOGETHER.

AS WE KISSED I FELT SO MANY THINGS!

THE CLOSER WE GOT, THE MORE STRESSED OUT I BECAME, UNTIL I FINALLY DUMPED HIM OVER MSN.

WHEN I WAS SIXTEEN, I GOT INTO MY FIRST REAL RELATIONSHIP. NOT SOME SILENT EXCHANGE OF MANGA, OR COVERT KISSING IN THE CINEMA, BUT A PROPER RELATIONSHIP. TALKS ABOUT *EMOTIONS*. DINNERS WITH PARENTS. *SLEEPOVERS*. IN THE *SAME BED*.

BUT FOR ALL THE "REALNESS" I THOUGHT THIS
RELATIONSHIP HAD, WE WERE STILL JUST TWO
SIXTEEN-YEAR-OLDS FIGURING THINGS OUT.

NO MATTER HOW MUCH TIME HE AND I SPENT
KISSING AND FUMBLING THROUGH
OUR TEENAGE HORMONES, I COULDN'T
HAVE SEX WITH HIM.

I FELT SO ISOLATED.
I KNEW PEOPLE WHO HADN'T HAD SEX, BUT
THAT WAS BECAUSE THEY HADN'T GOTTEN
BOYFRIENDS YET. IT SEEMED THAT NO ONE
WHO HAD A BOYFRIEND WAS STILL A VIRGIN.

IT GOT TO THE POINT WHERE I WAS SO
DISTRESSED AND CONFUSED I SPOKE TO MY
MUM ABOUT IT.

WE BROKE UP AFTER A YEAR.
I SPENT ABOUT A WEEK AVOIDING HIM AT SCHOOL,
CRYING IN THE STALLS WHEN I NEEDED TO
AND THEN I GOT OVER IT.

THE ONLY THING LEFT WAS TO FIND MYSELF AGAIN.
WHEN WE'D BEEN TOGETHER I'D CHANGED
SO MUCH.

BREAKING THE FOURTH WALL HERE: AUTOBIOGRAPHIES
ARE HARD BECAUSE IT MEANS LOOKING BACK AND
TRYING TO FIGURE STUFF OUT — I KNOW WHO I AM NOW,
BUT WHO WAS I THEN? AND QUEER MEMOIR IS
PARTICULARLY HARD!

CLOSED CLOSET →

CLOTHES RAIL ↥

PEOPLE MIGHT THINK THAT EVERYONE STARTS OUT IN A
CLOSET UNTIL THEY'RE READY TO "COME OUT." THE
CLOSET COULD BE DARK AND SCARY OR QUITE ROOMY
AND RESEMBLE MORE OF A CLOTHES RAIL. BUT WHAT'S
FUNNY FOR ME IS THAT I DIDN'T EVEN KNOW THAT THERE
<u>WAS</u> A CLOSET — OR THAT I WAS VERY MUCH STUCK
INSIDE IT.

FOUR

I WANTED TO REINVENT MYSELF.

BUT THAT DESIRE LED ME DOWN SOME DARK PATHS.

A DETERMINATION TO
GO FURTHER,
EAT LESS,
GET THINNER,
BE BETTER,
LOOK SEXIER,
BE DESIRABLE,
BE DESERVING.

ALTHOUGH I ONLY STARTED EXERCISING SERIOUSLY WHEN I WAS SEVENTEEN, I'D BEEN STUDYING MY BODY FOR YEARS.

I LOVE JEANS.

FROM THE AGE OF FOURTEEN UNTIL I WAS ABOUT TWENTY, I WAS HOLDING IN MY STOMACH.

111

WITHOUT REALIZING, I WAS STARTING TO CONTROL EVERYTHING ABOUT MY APPEARANCE, IDENTITY, AND LOVE LIFE.

I WANTED TO MAKE SURE I ARRIVED AT UNIVERSITY AS A REAL ADULT. I WAS SO DETERMINED TO BE OLDER, SKINNIER, COOLER!

MY STRUGGLE WITH FOOD WAS A
SUBCONSCIOUS WAY TO REDIRECT MYSELF
FROM THE FACT THAT I WAS GAY.

I CREATED A PROBLEM TO DISTRACT MY BRAIN
FROM MY BODY, A PASTIME FUELED WITH ANXIETY,
BUT ONE THAT WAS EASIER TO RECKON WITH THAN
ANY OF MY DEEPER, TRUER FEELINGS.

FIVE

I JUST COULDN'T HOLD ON TO THE PERSON I'D SPENT
SO MANY MONTHS PREPARING MYSELF TO BE.

IN MY HEAD I THOUGHT THAT BEING AT
UNIVERSITY WOULD LIFT AWAY THE THINGS THAT
HAD HELD ME BACK WHEN I WAS YOUNGER.
I WAS GOING TO STUDY ART, SOMETHING I'D
BEEN DREAMING OF FOR YEARS.
I WAS <u>MEANT</u> TO BE HERE.
THIS MEANT I'D BE A SOCIAL QUEEN,
I'D GO ON LOADS OF DATES,
AND MOST IMPORTANTLY —
I'D GET A BOYFRIEND.

MY FRIENDS AND I WOULD FRANTICALLY SCAN FACEBOOK, TRYING TO FIND THE HOTTEST BOYS IN OUR COURSE:

AND EVEN THOUGH I JOINED IN ON THIS MANIC HUNT, I WAS ALWAYS DISAPPOINTED. THE PIXELATED AND CROPPED FACES FROM THE BACKLIGHT OF MY LAPTOP DID NOTHING FOR ME.

I JUST DIDN'T CARE.

I WANTED TO BE KISSED, JUST NOT BY ANY OF THEM!

I WAS NERVOUS.

IF I DIDN'T MEET SOMEONE AT UNIVERSITY,
WHERE THE HELL WOULD I?

AND IF I WASN'T MEETING SOMEONE I LIKED,
WHAT ABOUT SEX?

SEX WAS QUICKLY BECOMING MORE
AND MORE TERRIFYING THE CLEARER IT
BECAME THAT I DIDN'T LIKE ANY
OF THE BOYS ENOUGH.

BEING AT SCHOOL HAD
PROTECTED ME SOMEWHAT.
BUT AT UNIVERSITY I WAS AN ADULT,
AND ADULTS HAVE SEX.

THAT SUMMER
I BEGAN WORKING AS A KITCHEN
RUNNER AT A BAR IN SOHO.

I PRETTY MUCH HATED WORKING THERE.

WORKING AT THIS BAR, I MET A WOMAN
CALLED ROSE.

DURING THE FIRST SHIFT I HAD WITH HER,
A MUCH OLDER CHEF LEANED OVER
THE COUNTER TO ME AND, NODDING
HIS HEAD TOWARDS ROSE,
BEGAN JAMMING HIS FINGERS
TOGETHER IN A SCISSORING
MOTION.

THE MEN IN THE KITCHEN WOULD OFTEN MAKE ME FEEL UNCOMFORTABLE.

ROSE NEVER SEEMED TO PAY ANY MIND TO
THESE WORDS OR GESTURES.
SHE BARELY LIFTED HER HEAD
IN RESPONSE.

AND I ALSO NEVER SPOKE OUT.

THE OTHER CHEFS' LANGUAGE WOULD
PARALYZE ME, LEAVE MY MIND FLIPPING.
I FELT SO ANGRY FOR HER BUT ALSO SO WORRIED
THAT IT MIGHT REVEAL SOMETHING ABOUT
ME IF I DEFENDED HER.

IT WAS AS THOUGH I BLACKED OUT AT EVERY
MENTION OF THE WORD "GAY" OR "LESBIAN."
MY MIND SIMPLY COULDN'T HANDLE IT.

A WEEK OR SO BEFORE I LEFT THAT JOB,
ROSE ALSO LEFT.

SHE ANNOUNCED IT QUITE SUDDENLY.
AT THE TIME, I WAS SO SAD,
I COULDN'T IMAGINE NOT HAVING HER
DOWNSTAIRS WITH ME, SHOWING ME HOW TO
SNAP THE WATERCRESS SO IT SAT ON THE
PLATE NEATLY, TALKING ME THROUGH THE WAY
THE FRIDGE WAS ARRANGED.

AFTER SHE LEFT, THE FRIDGE BECAME A SHORT
ESCAPE FOR ME DURING THOSE SHIFTS.
A MOMENT TO DULL OUT THE SOUND OF THE
REGISTER SENDING DOWN ORDERS,
A MOMENT TO COLLECT MY THOUGHTS AND
NOT HAVE TO BE IN A ROOM
FULL OF MEN.

THESE WERE OLDER MEN WHO WILL NEVER KNOW BETTER. IT WAS SIMPLY THE FIRST TIME I HAD EXPERIENCED MEN (NOT TEENAGE BOYS) TAKING SOMETHING FROM ME THAT THEY'D ALREADY DECIDED WAS THEIRS TO TAKE.

SIX

NEW YEAR'S EVE 2013

CECILIA, CAT, AND I WENT TO A FRIEND'S NEW YEAR'S EVE PARTY IN SOUTH LONDON. IT WAS A STRANGE MIXTURE OF PEOPLE I KNEW FROM SCHOOL, UP TO THOSE I'D MET AT UNIVERSITY.

SCENARIO:
I'M ABOUT TO COME OUT FOR THE
FIRST TIME.
DATE: 01/01/2014
TIME: 1:30 A.M.

I WENT TO SLEEP THAT NIGHT FEELING SO CONTENT,
SO CALM FOR THE FIRST TIME IN A WHILE.
I DON'T KNOW WHAT HAD HAPPENED DURING THAT
DAY TO HAVE BROUGHT THIS REALIZATION INTO MY MIND.

ALL I CAN PUT IT DOWN TO WAS THAT AFTER
YEARS OF TIRING MYSELF OUT WITH RULES
AND REGULATIONS, AN EVENING WITH MY
BEST FRIENDS MADE ME FEEL SO HAPPY AND
COMFORTABLE I FINALLY LET SOMETHING GO
AND THE TRUTH CAME OUT.

WHATEVER HAD CAUSED THIS TO HAPPEN,
IT COULDN'T LAST.

THE NEXT MORNING I AWOKE TO ANOTHER DAY
OF HETERONORMATIVITY.

I DIDN'T COME OUT AGAIN FOR A LONG
TIME AFTER THAT.

STORIES YOU HEAR ABOUT PEOPLE COMING OUT ARE OFTEN TOLD AS ONE BIG MOMENT. EVEN IF THE BUILD-UP HAS BEEN LONG AND PAINFUL — "COMING OUT" IS FREQUENTLY DESCRIBED AS A DEFINITIVE AND SINGULAR THING.

BUT IT DIDN'T HAPPEN LIKE THAT FOR *ME*.

MY COMING OUT WASN'T JUST A ONE-TIME THING, IT DIDN'T HAPPEN SO NEATLY. AFTER THIS FIRST COMING OUT IN FRONT OF *DONNY OSMOND AND HIS TECHNICOLOR DREAMCOAT*, IT TOOK ME TWO WHOLE YEARS TO COME OUT AGAIN.

IN 2015, I CAME OUT ANOTHER FOUR TIMES, WHICH WOULD MAKE IT A GRAND TOTAL OF FIVE.

WHEN I WAS NINETEEN I HAD SEX.

WE MET AT A DINNER
AND HE WAS REALLY NICE.

IN BED HE TOLD ME I WAS SEXY AND BEAUTIFUL AND I SAID NOTHING.

AFTERWARD HE GAVE ME HIS LAST CHOCOLATE BISCUIT BAR.

THE NEXT DAY I FELT TWO THINGS:

ONE WAS THAT I COULDN'T WAIT TO TELL MY
FRIEND IN THE ROOM DOWN THE HALL.

AND TWO WAS THAT I DIDN'T FEEL ANYTHING
ROMANTIC TOWARDS HIM ANYMORE.

AT THE TIME, I PUT MY CHANGE OF HEART DOWN TO
THE FACT THAT I SAW HIM IN SOCKS AND
FLIP-FLOPS.

IT WAS PRETTY COMMON FOR ME TO FIND SMALL,
SHALLOW REASONS NOT TO
HAVE THE HOTS FOR
A GUY ANYMORE.

IT COULD BE HIS NEW HAIRCUT,

OR THE FUZZY BEARD HE WAS TRYING TO GROW.

IN THE MOMENT, THESE REASONS FELT
EXTREMELY VALID.

SEVEN

A PANIC ATTACK STARTS WITH SHORTNESS
OF BREATH.

OR AT LEAST IT DID FOR ME.

MY VISION BEGAN TO TUNNEL
AND MY BREATHING QUICKENED.

IT WAS LIKE SEEING RED —
NOT THE RED OF ANGER
BUT THE RED OF EMERGENCY,
FLASHING SIRENS
TELLING EVERYONE TO
"GET OUT OF THE WAY!"

I HADN'T SAVED MY COURSEWORK PROPERLY.

I'D BEEN WORKING ON THE FILE FOR THREE MONTHS.

THE COURSEWORK WAS A PROGRAM FOR AN OPERA.

A DVOŘÁK OPERA ABOUT A WOMAN.

A WOMAN SO DESPERATE FOR THE LOVE OF A MAN SHE'S WILLING TO BE THE DEATH OF HIM.

I'M GOING TO FAIL.

I'M GOING TO FAIL MY DEGREE
AND IF I FAIL I HAVE TO CONFRONT
WHY I FAILED AND IF I CONFRONT
MY FAILURE I'LL UNDERSTAND WHY
I'VE FOUGHT SO HARD NOT TO FAIL.

IN THOSE THIRTY SECONDS
OF RED, THE CONTROL I HAD
FORCED INTO MY MIND, MY
BODY, AND UNDER MY SKIN
FINALLY BROKE.

THE NIGHT BEFORE MY FIRST SESSION
I TOOK A SMALL NOTEPAD FROM MY DESK
AND WROTE AT THE TOP OF A PAGE:
"THE WAVES ARE CRASHING AND CALLING."

SEEING MY COUNSELOR PULLED THOSE
WAVES BACK OUT TO SEA.

WE SPOKE ABOUT MY WORK AT UNIVERSITY,
MY FAMILY, THE WAY I FELT ABOUT MY BODY.
BUT I NEVER TOLD HER ABOUT THE FACT THAT
I HAD COME OUT AS GAY ON NEW YEAR'S EVE.

I DIDN'T TALK TO ANYONE ELSE ABOUT SEX, EITHER. SLEEPING WITH THAT GUY HADN'T OPENED UP THE WORLD OF SEX TO ME IN THE WAY I HAD EXPECTED. I WAS STILL VERY UNCOMFORTABLE WHEN CONFRONTED BY THE TOPIC.

I DID SPEAK TO THE COUNSELOR ABOUT BOYS, THOUGH.
I TOLD HER ABOUT GUYS THAT I THOUGHT WERE
NICE, BOYS THAT I FANCIED. BUT EVERY TIME SHE
ASKED ME HOW I REALLY FELT ABOUT IT ALL,
I'D BE HONEST AND SAY I DIDN'T REALLY CARE.

EIGHT

AT THE END OF MY FIRST YEAR, I MOVED INTO A FLAT WITH MY FRIENDS. IT WAS HERE THAT I STARTED TO REALIZE AGAIN THAT I WAS GAY. I'D BECOME MORE SETTLED AT ART SCHOOL AND BEEN EXPOSED TO A LOT MORE QUEER CULTURE THAN BEFORE.

AT THAT TIME, I MET SOMEONE WHO WAS
ALSO GOING THROUGH THE SAME PROCESS.
WE BECAME GOOD FRIENDS.

SHE HAD A BOYFRIEND, BUT WE'D OFTEN TALK ABOUT
THE GIRLS THAT SHE LIKED.

WE'D SOMETIMES HOLD HANDS. I'D MEET HER AFTER CLASS AND WE'D SPEND OUR EVENINGS TOGETHER.

ONCE AGAIN,
I FELT LIKE I HAD TWO SELVES: THE PERSON I WAS
WHEN I WAS AT UNIVERSITY, AND THE PERSON I WAS
WHEN I WAS WITH HER.

AT UNIVERSITY I'D TALK TO GIRLS IN MY CLASS
ABOUT BOYS, SCROLL THROUGH TINDER,
AND SET UP DATES.

WHEN WE WERE ALONE, IT FELT LIKE WE CREATED OUR
OWN BUBBLE. WE CLOSED THE DOOR ON ANYONE
WHO COULD POSSIBLY INTERFERE AND SPOKE ONLY
ABOUT EACH OTHER AND WHAT WE COULD BE.

EVEN WITH THIS FRIENDSHIP HAPPENING IN THE SIDELINES OF MY LIFE, I STILL NEVER SAID THAT I WAS GAY TO ANYONE ELSE. I THINK I WAS HOPING, MAYBE WAITING FOR HER TO BE READY TO SAY IT WITH ME. TOGETHER.
BUT SHE CHOSE TO STAY WITH HER BOYFRIEND AND I HAD TO COME OUT ALONE.

THE KNOWLEDGE BEGAN TO SOLIDIFY IN MY MIND
AND IT WOULD COME TO ME IN PRIVATE MOMENTS.

IT WASN'T SUCH AN EPIPHANY AS LAST TIME
WITH CAT AND CELI, IT WAS MORE LIKE

SMALL MOMENTS OF CLARITY,

LIKE I HAD TO TEST THE WORDS,
ALLOW THEM TO SETTLE INSIDE ME
BEFORE SPEAKING THEM ALOUD TO ANYONE ELSE.

ONE AFTERNOON, NEAR THE END OF SUMMER, MY BROTHER CAME BY TO HELP ME START MOVING MY THINGS OUT OF MY ROOM.

OUR LEASE WAS ALMOST UP AND I WANTED TO MOVE BACK HOME.

*MY BROTHER CALLS ME BIRD, BABY BIRD, BIRDUS, E-BIRD, B-BIRD, UCCELLINA (THAT'S ITALIAN FOR BABY GIRL BIRD).

TELLING HIM TURNED OUT TO BE EASIER
THAN TELLING MYSELF.

BUT FOR ALL MY EFFORTS, I STILL FOUGHT
AGAINST IT.

HE WAS *TALL!*
HE WAS *OLDER THAN ME!*
HE *ROCK CLIMBED!*
HE *HIKED!*
HE *COOKED!*
HE *HAD A JOB!*

HE WAS EVERYTHING I HAD
EVER SAID I WANTED IN A
BOYFRIEND, SO I
COULDN'T NOT GIVE
IT A GO.

BUT I HAD A PLAN.
IF OUR DATE DIDN'T GO WELL, THEN I WOULD
BE CERTAIN THAT I WAS
GAY.

MY LAST HETERO DATE

NINE

I REMEMBER THE MORNING AFTER THAT DATE
AND THE FEELING OF FINALLY KNOWING.
A DIFFERENT KNOWING THAN BEFORE. A DEFINITIVE
KNOWING, LIKE _THIS IS IT._

MY PARENTS WERE AWAY AND THE HOUSE WAS QUIET,
MY BROTHER WAS STILL SLEEPING IN THE ROOM
NEXT DOOR, SO I WENT FOR IT.

"I'M GAY."

IT WAS NEVER SOMETHING I'D SAID IN _MY HOUSE_ — I'D
ALWAYS BEEN SOMEWHERE ELSE: AT CECILIA'S, IN MY
FLAT, ON THE TUBE, ON THE STREET! I THREW THE
WORDS AROUND MY ROOM, A PLACE WHERE I HAD SLEPT
SINCE I WAS A BABY. THE WALLPAPER, DECORATIONS, AND
BEDDING HAD CHANGED OVER THE YEARS BUT THIS
ROOM WAS _MINE_. IT HAD HOUSED ME DURING ALL THIS
TIME, SO IT FELT RIGHT THAT IT WAS THE FIRST TO KNOW.

I LAY IN BED AND IMAGINED THE WORDS SQUEEZING OUT
FROM UNDER MY DOOR, FINDING THEMSELVES IN THE
HALLWAY AND SPLITTING OFF — SOME RAN INTO THE
BATHROOM AND LAID AGAINST THE COOL OF THE TILES,
OTHERS SLIPPED DOWNSTAIRS, SPILLING OVER THE
BANISTER AND SPLASHING UP THE WALLS OF MY
KITCHEN — THEY SPED INTO THE LIVING ROOM AND
PULLED OPEN THE BOOKS, TORE OUT THE WORDS AND
REPLACED THEM WITH ME. MY HOUSE AND I WERE
ROARING INTO NEW LIFE WHILE ALSO STAYING
EXACTLY THE SAME —
"I'M GAY."

TELLING MY HOUSE WASN'T SCARY,
IT COULDN'T TALK BACK.

I WAS NERVOUS ABOUT TELLING MY PARENTS, THOUGH.
IT WASN'T SOMETHING I'D EVER HAD TO PREPARE FOR
BECAUSE I'D NEVER HAD ANYTHING SOLID ENOUGH TO
TELL THEM. MY FEARS GREW FROM THE FEELING THAT
GAY WASN'T IN MY PARENTS' VOCABULARY. NOT BECAUSE
THEY WERE AGAINST IT BUT BECAUSE THEY'D NEVER
LIVED WITH IT. GAY, QUEER, LGBT+ WAS NOT A PART OF
THEIR DAILY LIVES AND SO THEY HAD RAISED ME IN AN
UNCONSCIOUSLY HETEROSEXUAL ENVIRONMENT.

IT WAS LIKE WHEN WE WATCHED *BUFFY THE VAMPIRE SLAYER* — MY PARENTS AND I LOVED WILLOW AND TARA'S RELATIONSHIP. *BUFFY* WAS A COOL FANTASY WORLD THAT WE DIPPED INTO WEEKLY. THE CHARACTERS WERE ACTION FIGURES, POSTERS, STICKERS, TRADING CARDS, AND PEOPLE I WOULD DRAW FOR MY OWN CHILDISH COMICS. BUT ONCE THE EPISODE WAS OVER, WE LEFT THE WORLD OF *BUFFY* AND WENT BACK TO "NORMAL LIFE."

WILLOW AND TARA WERE A PART OF THAT FICTIONAL WORLD, AND SO WAS THEIR RELATIONSHIP.

SO THOUGH I WAS DESPERATELY FINDING MYSELF IN EVERY ASPECT OF WILLOW, I NEVER EVEN CONSIDERED THAT THE BIGGEST PART OF HER CHARACTER — HER SEXUALITY — WAS THE MOST FUNDAMENTAL THING WE SHARED.

IT TURNED OUT THAT TELLING MY PARENTS WAS VERY EASY.

MY MUM AND I HAVE ALWAYS HAD A VERY TELEPATHIC RELATIONSHIP. IT'S FUNNY, BUT AT MOMENTS WHERE I'VE REALLY NEEDED HER, SHE'S READ MY MIND BEFORE I'VE EVEN SAID WHAT THE PROBLEM IS.

LIKE THAT TIME WHEN I WAS AN EMBARRASSED SIXTEEN-YEAR-OLD (PRE-EMPTIVE IN MY CONTRACEPTIVE REQUIREMENTS).

OR THAT TIME I HIT A ROAD BUMP AT HIGH SPEED, FLINGING MYSELF OFF THE BIKE AND BREAKING MY WRIST. IT LOOKED LIKE A POTATO.

AND THIS TIME WAS NO DIFFERENT.

AFTER THAT, TELLING THE REST OF MY
FAMILY WAS SIMPLE.

TEN

I FELT LIKE MY BODY WAS IN SHOCK.
ALL THE WAYS I HAD TRIED TO EXPRESS MYSELF
AND CONTROL MY IMAGE FELL AWAY BECAUSE
I HAD *FINALLY* TOLD THE TRUTH.

I SUDDENLY HAD THIS NEW BURST OF LIFE.
I WAS TWENTY-ONE WITH TWENTY-ONE YEARS OF
QUEER CULTURE TO CATCH UP ON — OH BABY!

I GOT TO LOOK AT MYSELF IN THIS WHOLE OTHER LIGHT. THE ONE QUESTION I HAD SEARCHED AND TORN MYSELF UP OVER WAS *ANSWERED!*

I STILL FLIPPED AROUND A LOT FROM MOMENTS
OF RELIEF TO FEELINGS OF

IT WAS VERY STRANGE TO KNOW THAT UNTIL THEN I HAD
LIVED MY LIFE AS A DIFFERENT PERSON, WITH THOUGHTS
TAKEN UP BY BOYS AND FOOD AND HOW TO BE. I FEARED
I HAD MISSED OUT ON WHO I COULD HAVE BEEN HAD I
KNOWN EARLIER.

BUT SCREW THAT!

I DELETED TINDER – THANK GOD!

I STARTED DATING AGAIN — HELLO, LONDON!

ALL THINGS GAY AND BEAUTIFUL WERE SPILLING
INTO MY LIFE AND CHANGING MY HAIR, MY CLOTHES,
THE BOOKS I READ, AND THE WAY I WORKED.
MY EXCITEMENT AND INSPIRATION DIMINISHED
ANY FEARS I HELD ABOUT WHAT I HAD LOST IN THOSE
LONG YEARS OF FALSE HETERO HELL.

SO BASICALLY, THE TRIPTYCH WILL PORTRAY THE SUBTLE YET DISTINCTLY QUEER RELATIONSHIP BETWEEN NELL AND THEO IN SHIRLEY JACKSON'S *THE HAUNTING OF HILL HOUSE*, AND HOW THAT RELATIONSHIP REALLY SEEMS TO PAIR WITH NELL'S MENTAL POSSESSION FROM THE HOUSE, WHICH IS, IN AND OF ITSELF, A MALEVOLENT SPIRIT. WAS IT A SOCIAL COMMENT AT THE TIME REGARDING THE DISBELIEF AND THEREFORE ERASURE OF QUEER WOMEN THAT URGED JACKSON TO LEAD OUR ANTI-HERO NELL TO SEEMINGLY COMMIT SUICIDE RATHER THAN LEAVE HILL HOUSE FOR GOOD, WHEN THE READER THEMSELF KNOWS IT WAS THE HOUSE THAT WAS CONTROLLING HER THE WHOLE TIME?

THANK YOU, ELLIE.

I RETURNED TO MY UNIVERSITY FOR THE THIRD AND FINAL YEAR OF MY DEGREE AND IT WAS LIKE I'D STARTED OVER AGAIN. RATHER THAN SIMPLY CATCHING UP ON SUMMER EVENTS WITH MY FRIENDS, I GOT TO REINTRODUCE MYSELF AS THE "REAL ME" BY COMING OUT. IT FELT LIKE I'D BEEN WASHED CLEAN.

ELEVEN

THE FIRST DATE I EVER HAD WITH A WOMAN WENT LIKE THIS:

WE AGREED TO MEET AT A
PING-PONG BAR
AND I WORE
MY NEW SHOES.

WHEN I ARRIVED WE GOT A PINT
AND SHE TOLD ME THAT I HAD
SO MANY DIFFERENT HAIRSTYLES
IN MY PROFILE PHOTOS, SHE
WASN'T SURE WHAT I ACTUALLY
LOOKED LIKE.

WHOOPS!

HEH

WE HAD A FEW MORE DRINKS, ATE SOME PIZZA,
AND WALKED TO THE STATION.

SHE TEXTED ME TWO DAYS LATER SAYING THAT
WE WEREN'T "LOOKING FOR THE SAME THINGS."

MY NEW SHOES HAD
GIVEN ME BLISTERS.

SALT WATER
FOR MY FEET →

BUT IT ONLY GOT
WORSE WITH THE
SECOND DATE...

WE MET AT A WINE BAR AND SHE CALLED ME A "BABY GAY" WHEN SHE REALIZED I'D ONLY COME OUT RECENTLY.

SHE THEN ORDERED US A LONG AND EXPENSIVE TAXI ACROSS LONDON TO A DIFFERENT BAR, WHERE WE RAN INTO HER FRIENDS WHO WERE GOING TO A PARTY.

AFTER SOME MORE DRINKS, SHE DECIDED SHE WAS GOING TO GO TO THAT PARTY AND THAT I SHOULDN'T COME WITH HER, AS HER EX-GIRLFRIEND WOULD BE THERE AND SHE WANTED TO SCOPE IT OUT FIRST.

IT'S 2 AM

WE CAN MEET UP AGAIN LATER.

I THREW UP WHEN I GOT HOME.

I WON'T LIE, I WAS SHOCKED.
I'D BEEN SO EXCITED ABOUT COMING OUT THAT I HAD
FORGOTTEN THAT THIS WOULDN'T MAKE DATING
SUDDENLY EASIER. I STILL HAD TO CONNECT WITH THE
PEOPLE I MET.

MY DATING EXPERIENCE HAD CONSISTED OF ME FORCING OR MISJUDGING CONNECTIONS AS ROMANTIC. I'D HAD NO EXPERIENCE OF A GENUINE SPARK OF ATTRACTION.

I DIDN'T EVEN KNOW HOW TO FLIRT!

HOWEVER HARD IT WOULD GET,
I DECIDED THIS TIME I WOULD MAKE NO PLANS,
NO RULES OR REGULATIONS.
I WAS JUST GOING TO ENJOY MYSELF
AND KEEP TRYING.

269

AND THEN, I SAW HER.

TWELVE

I MET T AT A PUB IN NORTH LONDON.

WE SPOKE NONSTOP FOR FOUR HOURS,
AND AS THE PUB CLOSED SHE WALKED ME
TO MY BUS STOP AND WE TALKED ABOUT
OUR FAMILIES.

AS MY BUS ARRIVED TO GO HOME, SHE HOPPED ON TO HER BIKE AND PEDALED AWAY, CALLING GOODBYE OVER HER SHOULDER.

WE HAD SPOKEN ABOUT A BOOK WE WERE BOTH
READING AND THE WRITER WAS GIVING A TALK
IN A FEW WEEKS' TIME.

WE AGREED TO GO TOGETHER AS OUR SECOND DATE.

AFTER ABOUT FIVE DATES I KNEW IT WAS TIME
FOR US TO KISS, BUT I WAS SO SCARED!
I HAD KISSED GIRLS BEFORE, BUT NEVER IN
A ROMANTIC WAY. NEVER IN A WAY THAT WAS
MEANT TO MAKE THEM WANT TO KISS ME AGAIN.
AND I REALLY WANTED T TO KISS ME AGAIN!

AFTER THAT WE BEGAN TO SEE EACH OTHER
REGULARLY EACH WEEK AND I STOPPED
ASKING OTHER GIRLS OUT ON DATES. THIS WASN'T
SOMETHING WE'D AGREED ON, IT JUST FELT RIGHT,
AND IT TURNED OUT SHE HAD MADE THE SAME CHOICE.

THIRTEEN

AFTER I GRADUATED FROM UNIVERSITY, I WENT TO TORONTO FOR TWO WEEKS WITH MY PARENTS.
I'D ALWAYS WANTED TO VISIT CANADA, AND THIS WAS A TRIP I'D BEEN PLANNING FOR A LONG TIME.

BUT ONCE I WAS THERE I COULDN'T CONCENTRATE.

I MISSED T SO MUCH.
WE'D BEEN DATING FOR ALMOST NINE MONTHS
WITH HARDLY ANY TIME APART,
TWO WEEKS FELT LIKE A LIFETIME.

I REMEMBER WALKING DOWN THE STREET
WITH MY MUM ONE AFTERNOON OF OUR TRIP
WHEN T SENT ME A DEMO FOR HER SONG.

SHE WAS SO RIGHT.

WE CALLED A FEW DAYS LATER AND BOOKED A TRIP TO BARCELONA. I ENJOYED THE REST OF MY HOLIDAY BUT WAS SECRETLY COUNTING DOWN THE DAYS.

THE MOMENT I GOT BACK TO MY
HOUSE IN LONDON I THREW MY CLOTHES
IN A BAG, GRABBED THE PRESENTS I'D
BOUGHT FOR T, AND JUMPED
IN A TAXI.

A FEW WEEKS LATER, WE SET OFF ON OUR FIRST HOLIDAY TOGETHER.

ONE EVENING ON THAT TRIP, AFTER AN EVENTFUL DINNER WHERE THE FOOD WAS COLD AND I'D KNOCKED OVER A TABLE, SPILLING CHILLI SAUCE ACROSS THE FLOOR, T ASKED ME TO BE HER GIRLFRIEND.

YEAH, WE'D BEEN DATING FOR NEARLY A YEAR BUT WE'D AGREED TO TAKE THINGS AT OUR OWN PACE. IT FELT SO PERFECT AND RIGHT WHEN T ASKED ME THAT NIGHT. WE WALKED BACK HOME HOLDING HANDS, LAUGHING ABOUT THE DINNER AND SINGING.

EPILOGUE

BEFORE I STARTED SEEING A COUNSELOR, I HAD TO COMPLETE AN ASSESSMENT TO DETERMINE WHAT I NEEDED. THE WOMAN WHO TOOK ME THROUGH IT WAS SCOTTISH, WITH FRECKLES AND FLUFFY BROWN HAIR.

I CAN'T REMEMBER EVERYTHING SHE ASKED ME, BUT ONE OF THE QUESTIONS ALWAYS STUCK IN MY MIND AFTERWARD.
SHE SAID:

WHEN YOU THINK OF YOUR CHILDHOOD

WHAT DO YOU SEE?

AND I SAID:

ORANGE LIKE MY HAIR — ORANGE LIKE THE SUN SEEN THROUGH CLOSED EYELIDS.

WHEN I CAME OUT THAT FINAL
TIME IN MY ROOM, THE BIGGEST
KNOT I HAVE EVER CARRIED
IN MY LIFE CAME UNDONE.

OF COURSE, THERE
HAVE SINCE BEEN
– THERE ARE –
AND THERE WILL BE
OTHER KNOTS.

BUT WHEN I REALIZED HOW I NEEDED TO LIVE
MY LIFE, I BECAME MORE FEARLESS ABOUT
THEM ALL.

319

ABOUT THE AUTHOR
ELEANOR CREWES IS A LONDON-BASED
ILLUSTRATOR AND AUTHOR WHO GRADUATED
FROM THE UNIVERSITY OF THE ARTS LONDON.

THE DRAWINGS IN THIS BOOK WERE RENDERED USING
PALOMINO PEARL PENCILS.